COMMUNITY SCHOOL
RARY
26.5.95
KV-399-751

003428

Titles in the Migrations series

African Migrations
Chinese Migrations
Indian Migrations
Jewish Migrations

Dedication
To Omar Alghali, Reuben and Hannah, with love.

Acknowledgements
Grateful thanks to the following people for their support and helpful comments: Omar Alghali, Ann Clarke, John Sellars, Kaye Stearman and Rozina Visram.

First published in 1994 by Wayland (Publishers) Ltd
61 Western Road, Hove, East Sussex, BN3 1JD, England

Editor: Cath Senker
Series design: Suzie Hooper
Book design: Pardoe Blacker Ltd
Cover design: Simon Borrough
Production controller: Janet Slater

British Library Cataloguing in Publication Data
Warner, Rachel
Indian Migrations (Migrations series)
I. Title II. Series
305.891

ISBN 0-7502-1077-X

Printed and bound in Italy by G. Canale & C.S.p.A., Turin

Links with the National Curriculum

HISTORY
KS 2 Core Unit 4: Britain since 1930
Especially chapter 7, which looks at social changes in Britain.

KS 2 Extension Studies A: Ships and Seafarers
Especially chapter 5.

KS 3 Core Unit 3: Expansion, Trade and Industry – Britain 1750 to 1900
Especially chapters 2 and 3, which look at Britain's world-wide expansion.
Core Unit 4: The Twentieth-Century World

KS 3 Supplementary Unit B: a unit involving the study of a past non-European society, for example, India.

GEOGRAPHY
KS 2 Communications: Journeys
KS 3 Places: Asia
Population: Migration

The cross-curricular theme of Citizenship, particularly component 2: A Pluralist Society, and also component 3: Being a Citizen.

CONTENTS

World map showing Indian migrations 4
1 Migrations in ancient times 6
2 Indian professionals migrate in the 1800s 10
3 Indians leave as indentured labourers 18
4 Moving as traders - and as refugees 26
5 The lascars sail overseas 30
6 Indians flee as refugees 36
7 Migrating to work abroad after 1947 41
Glossary 46
Find out more 47
Notes on sources 48
Index 48

Note: About one in four people in the world today live in the Indian subcontinent. Until 1947 the term India covered the whole area but today it is divided into three independent countries - India, Pakistan and Bangladesh. Within this huge area, there are many different peoples, languages and religions. Some of the peoples mentioned in this book are Bengalis (from Bangladesh and east India), Tamils (from south India), Gujaratis (from west India) and Punjabis (from north India and Pakistan).

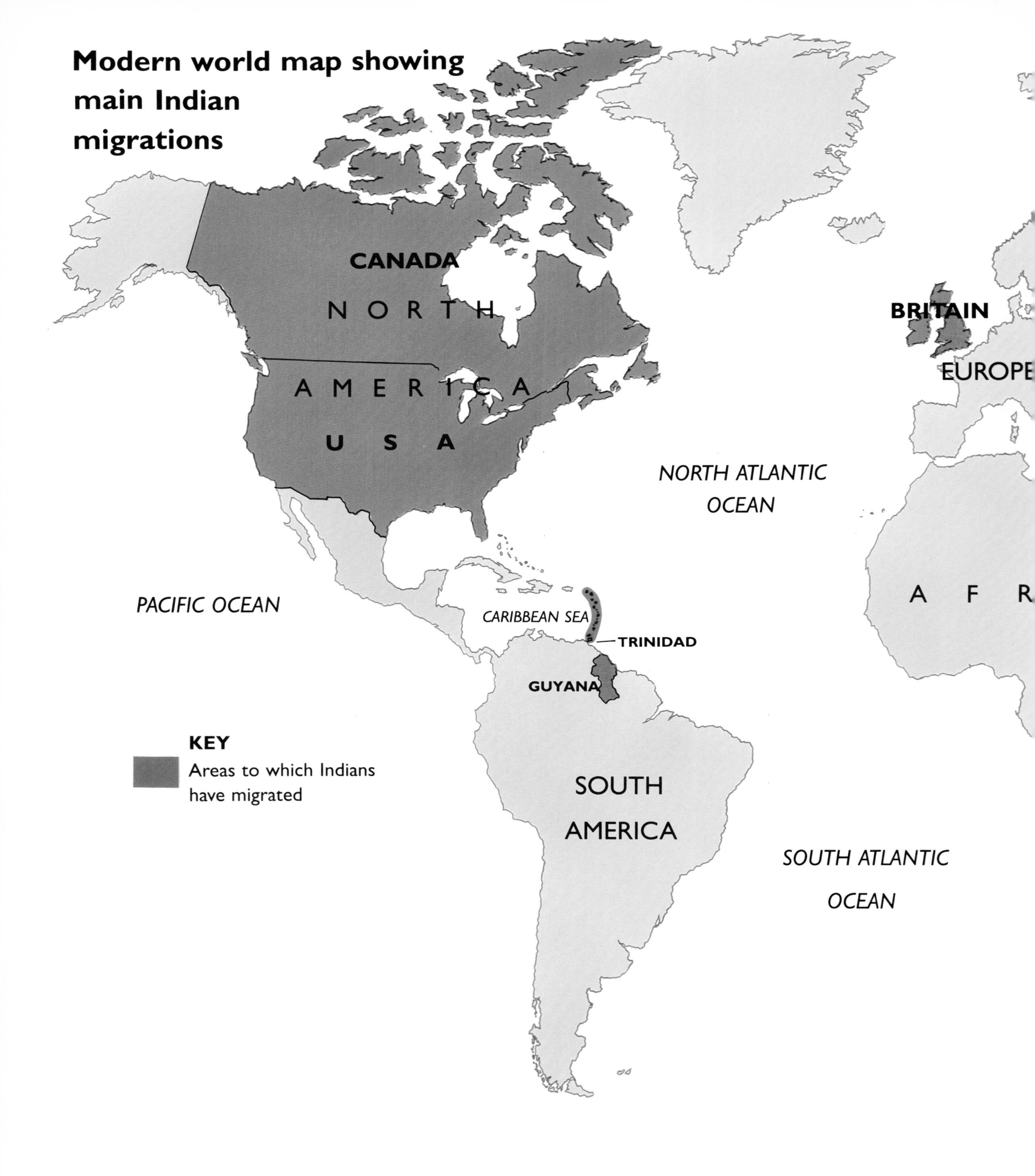
Modern world map showing main Indian migrations
CANADA
NORTH AMERICA
USA
BRITAIN
EUROPE
NORTH ATLANTIC OCEAN
PACIFIC OCEAN
CARIBBEAN SEA
TRINIDAD
GUYANA
KEY
Areas to which Indians have migrated
SOUTH AMERICA
SOUTH ATLANTIC OCEAN

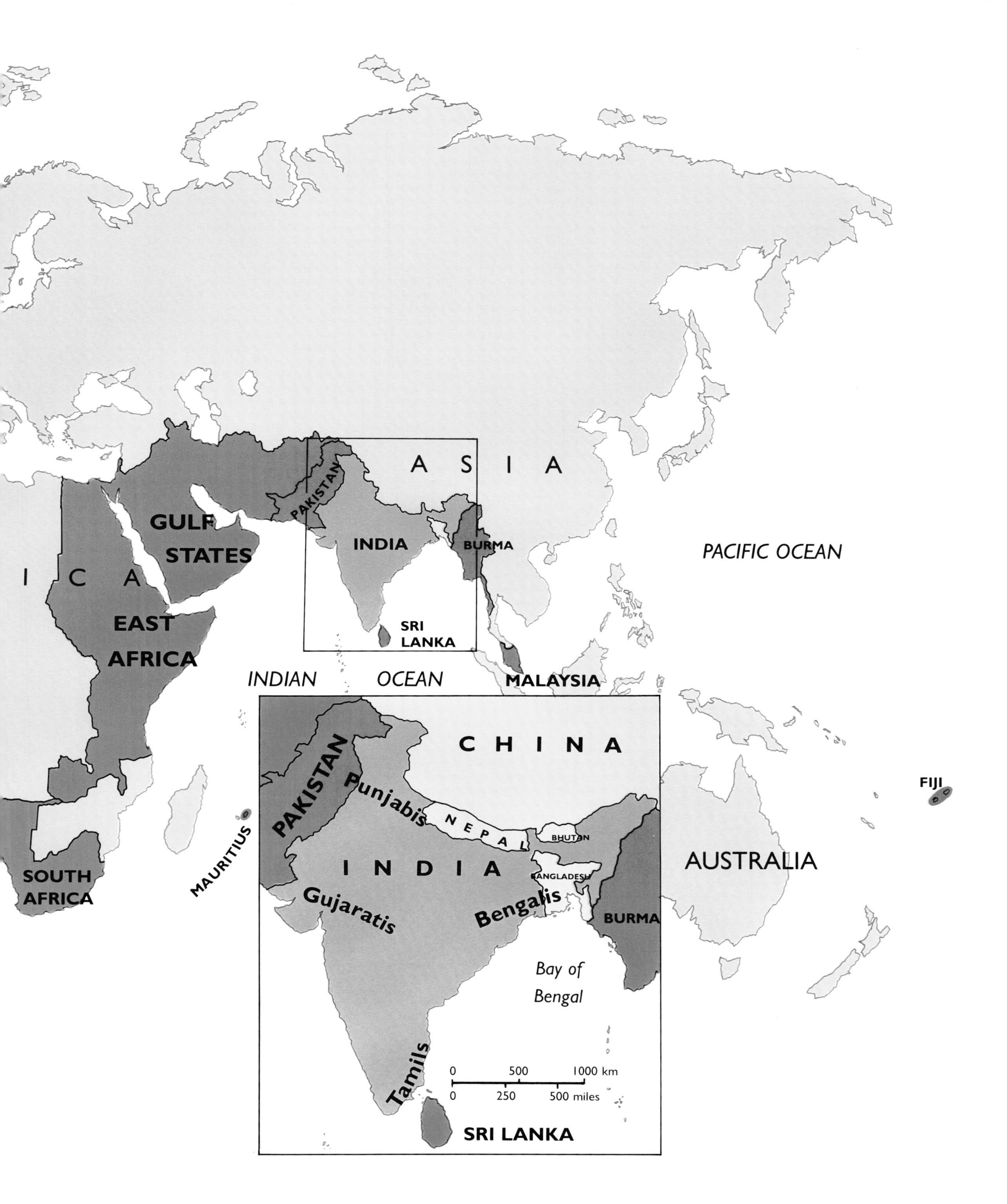

A S I A
PACIFIC OCEAN
I C A
GULF STATES
EAST AFRICA
PAKISTAN
INDIA
BURMA
SRI LANKA
INDIAN
OCEAN
MALAYSIA
SOUTH AFRICA
MAURITIUS
FIJI
AUSTRALIA
C H I N A
PAKISTAN
Punjabis
N E P A L
BHUTAN
I N D I A
BANGLADESH
Gujaratis
Bengalis
BURMA
Bay of Bengal
Tamils
0 500 1000 km
0 250 500 miles
SRI LANKA

1 Migrations in ancient times

Introduction

People migrate when they move from one place to another to live. They move for many different reasons. Sometimes they choose to migrate and move willingly. Other people go reluctantly, while sometimes they are forced to leave their homes.

Many countries in the world today have Indian communities. Indians have migrated throughout the long history of India; not just in the twentieth century. People have also migrated from one part of India to another – for example, from the countryside to the big cities like Bombay, Calcutta and Delhi in search of work.

In Dhaka, the capital of Bangladesh, some of the people who have come to the city looking for work live in slums like this beside the railway track.

In ancient times, Indians left India as travellers, adventurers and conquerors. They also spread the religions of India – especially Buddhism – to other countries, for example, China.

One of the places Indians went to in ancient times was Sri Lanka, or Ceylon as it was called until 1972. Sri Lanka is an island close to the south of India. There are two main groups of people living in Sri Lanka today – the Sinhalese and the Tamils. Both groups originally came from India. The Sinhalese are the descendants of people who migrated from north India and the Ceylon Tamils descend from people who originally migrated from south India.

A Tamil tea picker in Sri Lanka today.

The story of Prince Vijaya

One of the ancient stories of Sri Lanka, called the *Mahavamsa*, tells how Prince Vijaya went to Sri Lanka from north India in the fifth century BC. He was sent away by his father because he behaved so badly, and was put to sea in a ship with 700 followers. The group landed in Sri Lanka as the first Indian migrants. According to the story, demons lived on the island. Vijaya and his followers defeated the demons and Vijaya married a demon princess called Kuveni. Later, Vijaya drove Kuveni away because he felt she wasn't good enough to be his queen. He sent messengers to India to bring an Indian princess to be his wife. Vijaya called his new kingdom 'Sinhala', which means 'lion', because his grandfather was a lion.

Although this is a legend it contains the basic facts about how the Sinhalese arrived in Sri Lanka.

The story of the *Ramayana*

Another ancient story which includes a journey to Sri Lanka (or Lanka as it was called) is the *Ramayana*. The *Ramayana* is one of the great stories of the Hindu religion in India. It was written in Sanskrit in about the third century BC, and it mentions the ancient Tamil kingdoms of Sri Lanka. Although the story is ancient, it is still popular with Indians all over the world and has been made into a hugely successful series on Indian TV. Wherever Hindu Indians have migrated they have taken the story of the *Ramayana* with them. The *Ramayana* is celebrated in the Indian festivals of *Dussehra* and *Divali*.

Sita and Rama (seated), Lakshman behind, with Hanuman in front.

Rama and Lakshman searching for Sita after Ravan had taken her away.

The story takes place in north India. Prince Rama and his beautiful wife Sita were sent away to the forest for fourteen years. Ravan, the ten-headed demon king of Lanka, tricked Sita while Rama was away and carried her off to his capital in Lanka. Rama and his brother Lakshman tried to rescue Sita. With the help of the monkey-general Hanuman they attacked Lanka and in a terrible fight Rama killed the wicked Ravan. He rescued Sita and took her back to India.

SRI LANKA TODAY

The population of Sri Lanka in 1992 was about 17.5 million. 18 per cent of the people are Tamils and 74 per cent are Sinhalese. (The rest include Muslims and other groups.) The Sinhalese are mainly Buddhist and speak Sinhala; the Tamils are mainly Hindu and speak Tamil. As well as the Ceylon Tamils who have been in Sri Lanka since ancient times, there are also Tamils who came from India in the nineteenth century to work on the tea plantations of Sri Lanka.

(Right) A young Tamil fighter.

Tamil workers in a factory in Sri Lanka.

Although both the Sinhalese and the Tamils originally came from India, today the two groups are in conflict. From the nineteenth century, Britain ruled Sri Lanka as a colony, and the Sinhalese feel that the British gave the Tamils more privileges. However, the Tamils have felt that since independence from Britain in 1948 the Sinhalese have been deliberately discriminating against them. In despair, many Tamils decided that their only hope lay in fighting for a separate state of Eelam in the north and east of the island. The fighting beween the Sinhalese and Tamils has led to thousands of deaths and many Tamils leaving Sri Lanka as refugees.

2 Indian professionals migrate in the 1800s

Britain used to rule over a large empire. This was made up of other countries that Britain ruled, called colonies. Britain ruled India as one of its colonies.

India had been a rich and prosperous land; beautiful cloth was woven there, and India also sold sugar, spices and indigo (a blue dye) abroad. European countries were keen to have some of India's riches.

Britain started to control its trade with India through the British East India Company, which was established in 1600.

This Indian illustration from 1590 shows the different stages of preparing wool to make cloth.

A painting showing the attack by British soldiers on the city of Delhi in May 1857.

Gradually, however, the East India Company became more interested in controlling parts of India, not just in trading. The Mogul Empire, which ruled India at that time, had become weak, so it was reasonably easy for the East India Company to take control of the country. By the 1850s, the British Army had conquered large parts of India and many British people went there to run the country as police officers, soldiers, lawyers, tax collectors and civil servants. In 1857 some Indians revolted against British rule in India. The British put this revolt down with great cruelty. Afterwards, in 1858, India was ruled directly as a colony by Queen Victoria and her government in London.

One of the effects of British rule in India was the introduction of the English language and the British education system. From the middle of the nineteenth century, Indian students began arriving in Britain to study – law and medicine in particular. Some went to take the entry examination for the Indian civil service so that they could take part in running their country alongside British people. It was only possible to take the examination in London. This discriminated against Indians as it was only those who could afford to go to London who could take the examination.

Jawaharlal Nehru (fifth from the right, second row from the back) at Harrow School, London, England in 1907.

The first Indian students arrived in Britain in 1845. By 1880 there were about 100 of them studying in Britain. This number rose to 700 by 1910 and to 1,800 in 1931. Many famous Indians were students in Britain – for example, Mohandas Karamchand Gandhi (see p.15), Muhammad Ali Jinnah (the founder of Pakistan), Jawaharlal Nehru (independent India's first prime minister) and his daughter, Indira Gandhi (Prime Minister of India from 1966–77 and from 1980–84).

Instead of going back to India, some Indian students settled in Britain after they had finished studying. They worked as teachers, university professors, doctors, lawyers and in other professional jobs. Other professional Indians went to Britain to work for Indian businesses which had opened branches there.

A photograph of Cornelia Sorabji, a very educated Indian woman who came to study law at Somerville College, Oxford in 1888.

Dadabhai Naoroji

Dadabhai Naoroji, later to be Britain's first Asian Member of Parliament, came from Bombay. There, he had been a professor of mathematics. He went to Britain in 1855 to set up the firm of Cama and Co., which dealt in cotton. He later set up his own cotton company and worked for some time as Professor of Gujarati at London University. Although he was a businessman, Naoroji's main interest in life was to criticize British rule in India.

He made many speeches and wrote books about how the British Raj (government) exploited India. For example, the British destroyed the Indian cotton industry so that Indians had to buy expensive cotton goods from Britain. India was made to produce the raw materials the British needed for their own industries - like cotton, tea, indigo and jute - rather than food to feed the people of India.

Naoroji's election address in 1895. Although popular with local people, he lost the seat of Central Finsbury for the Liberals in 1895.

Naoroji also criticized the way Indians had little part in the running of their country; he said that the Indian civil service examinations should be held in India as well as England so that Indians had more chance of taking them. Eventually Naoroji decided that he should enter parliament in Britain so he could speak out about the sufferings of Indians - who were, after all, British subjects. He won the seat of Central Finsbury in London for the Liberal Party in 1892 and so became the first ever Asian Member of Parliament (MP). At last, the people of India had one voice in the British parliament speaking for them. He remained an MP for three years.

The plantation owners then needed other people who would work very cheaply on their plantations, in place of the freed slaves.

They turned to India, as another British colony, for these labourers. The people in India (mainly men) who agreed to go to work on the plantations in different British colonies were very poor – often starving. Their poverty was caused partly by the way the British had destroyed traditional Indian industries. Many more people went overseas to work as indentured labourers in the years when there was famine in the part of India they lived in. It was poverty in India that pushed people to leave; it was not because they wanted to go.

Indeed, many people were forced to go or were even kidnapped by recruiting agents. As indentured labourers they were not much different to slaves. The indenture meant they had to work on the plantation for five years and they belonged to their new employer for that time. They had no rights and were treated very badly.

Indians went to Mauritius, Fiji, Natal in South Africa, the Caribbean (mainly Trinidad), Guyana, Malaysia, Burma and Sri Lanka to work as indentured labourers on plantations. The Indian communities in these countries today are mainly descendants of indentured labourers who went there in the past.

Indians waiting to leave for Fiji as indentured labourers (or 'coolies' as they were sometimes known).

An indentured labourer in Trinidad tells his story:

'I used to own a little bit of land in my village in India and I grew rice and chillies for my family. But then the rains failed for two years in a row and we had nothing left to eat. So I sold my land. What else could I do? I worked on other people's fields in exchange for rice but I could never get enough to feed my family. I owed the moneylender lots of money which I could never pay back. Then one day a strange man arrived in our village. He said there were lots of jobs for people like me across the sea, the black water that brings us bad luck if we cross it. He said I could cut sugar cane and if I went I would soon be able to earn enough money to pay off my debts and come back a rich man. I was a bit suspicious – it seemed too good to be true – but I and thirty other men and two young widows from the village agreed to go.

'I said a tearful goodbye to my wife. She begged me not to go but I told her I would be back in a few years. Little did I know that I would never see her again. We had to walk to Calcutta where the man told us we would get our ship. What he didn't tell us was how far it was. It took nearly forty days to get there and I must say our spirits flagged. Was this really going to be any better?

Indentured labourers boarding their ship in Calcutta.

'I couldn't believe how noisy Calcutta was when we arrived. So many people! And such big buildings! I had never seen a city before. We were taken to a big building by the river and were allowed to rest for a few weeks. I was told we were going to somewhere called Trinidad, a long way across the sea. I'd never heard of it before. They said that it would get cold on the journey, especially round somewhere called the Cape of Good Hope, so they gave us a set of warm clothes. I couldn't imagine needing such clothes while I was in the incredible heat of Calcutta.

'I'd seen all the huge sailing ships moored along the Hooghly River and finally it was my turn to board one. I said a silent goodbye to India as I turned for a last look at Calcutta. I must say the white sails of the ship were splendid as they billowed in the wind.

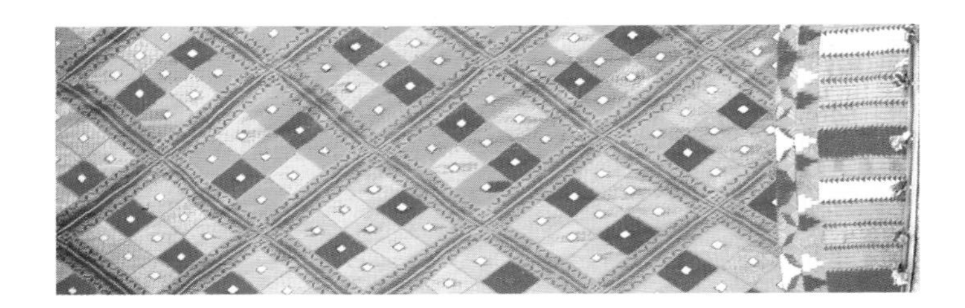

'We were at sea for over three months. The journey was terrible and I was lucky to arrive alive. Two people killed themselves on the journey. Eleven people from my village died from cholera on the way. The ship was crowded, the food was awful and it was very difficult to keep clean. Many people were ill before we even started the voyage. I felt miserable but was relieved to be off the ship when we finally arrived in Trinidad.' [1]

What work did Indian indentured labourers do?

An indentured labourer in Fiji tells his story:

'I came to Fiji in 1890 to cut sugar-cane. Although most Indians in Fiji speak Hindi and are from north India, I'm a Tamil and I came on a steamship from Madras in south India. I'm a Brahmin, a Hindu religious man, and had never worked in the fields before – I told them I had, because I was desperate to get work. They didn't bother to check my hands – if they had they'd have seen I'd never done manual work before.

Indian labourers breaking cocoa pods in Trinidad in about 1890.

INDIANS IN TRINIDAD TODAY

Forty per cent of the population of Trinidad today are Indian. They are mainly descendants of the indentured labourers. When the period of indenture was over it was possible for the labourers to return to India. However, many chose to take land in Trinidad instead, as it would have been much harder to get land back in India. Many Indians in Trinidad today are still farmers. The Indians of Trinidad are clearly different to the Creoles (or Afro-Caribbeans) in their religions, the food they eat and their life style. But during their time in Trinidad many of their customs have also changed.

One of the most famous Indians of Trinidad is the novelist, V.S. Naipaul.

(Above) Farm worker in Trinidad today, descended from Indian indentured labourers. (Left) V.S. Naipaul.

'I couldn't believe how hard the work was on the sugar plantation. We had to plant the cane, to weed the ground, and hardest of all, to cut the cane. In the harvest season we worked day and night to get the cane to the sugar mill. Sometimes I thought I was going to drop with exhaustion. I'd come to Fiji to earn money, yet often my wages were stopped for not finishing the job or for breaking something. We lived in miserable huts in long lines – but you should have seen the plantation owner's house! It was enormous. The only thing that kept me going in those early days was the thought of a drink in the evening, or celebrating one of our Hindu festivals.' [2]

INDIANS IN FIJI TODAY

The islands of Fiji are in the South Pacific. Indians form 50 per cent of the population of Fiji today and are Fijian citizens. Descendants of the indentured labourers from India live side by side with Fijian islanders, yet the two groups mix very little. When Fiji became independent from Britain in 1970, the Fijians were given more power in the political system than the Indians. This has led to racial tension between the two groups.

In the late 1980s and early 1990s the Fijians seized even more political power and Indians in Fiji have become afraid for their future. Many Indian professionals have emigrated to other countries – particularly Canada and Australia, but it is hard for poor people to leave. The Indians have lost contact with India because their families have lived in Fiji for a hundred years.

Indian women in Fiji, about 1960.

Indentured labourers were also used in the late 1890s to build the Uganda Railway for the British Empire in East Africa. The railway was over 950 km long and ran from Mombasa on the coast (in present-day Kenya) to Lake Victoria in Uganda. A railway worker who came to Africa from the area that is now Pakistan tells his story:

'I can see why the local Africans don't want to work on this railway. We've built about 120 miles [200 km] so far, and I can feel every mile in my aching body. I work in the gang that puts the sleepers down once the ground has been cleared. The sleepers are very heavy and we have to work quickly because the next gang is behind us putting the rail lengths down. Another gang join the track sections together and another lot fix the rail to the sleepers.

'It's very hard work. We live in tents which we take with us when the railway moves forwards. Many of us have been ill with malaria and dysentery, and the heat is incredible.

'The most frightening thing has just happened. We had just built a temporary bridge over the River Tsavo when one of the men simply disappeared without trace. Our white boss, Mr Preston, went to look for him. He found the missing man's body – ripped to pieces by a lion. We are all terrified, stuck in this god-forsaken place with a man-eating lion stalking about out there.' [3]

The tents that the Indian labourers lived in while they built the Uganda Railway.

The Uganda Railway was finished in 1903, after seven years. Of the 32,000 Indians brought to work on it, most went back to India once it was finished. Many had died before they could return.

Indian platelaying gangs who laid the tracks of the Uganda Railway.

4 Moving as traders – and as refugees

0 500 1000 1500 km
0 200 400 600 800 1000 miles

A F R I

Other Indians soon followed the indentured labourers, mainly to African countries. They were called 'free immigrants', or 'passengers'. Unlike the indentured labourers who went unwillingly and had to work for five years for the same employer, these Indians went freely and paid their own travelling costs. They were mainly from Gujarat and Punjab.

The 'free immigrants' went to earn a living through trade - by running small shops and businesses. There had been some Indian traders in East Africa long before the nineteenth century, but many 'passengers' now followed the railway workers to East Africa.

Gulshan (wearing glasses) in African dress.

All over Uganda, Kenya, Tanzania, Malawi and Zambia Indian-run shops and businesses became a common sight. Other Indians found work as clerks in offices, on the railways and in the postal service.

Gulshan Parekh, who was born in 1938, tells her story:

'My father left Gujarat in 1914 for Uganda. My grandfather had lots of children and he didn't have enough land for all of them. So the sons had to find some other way of making a living, instead of farming the land.

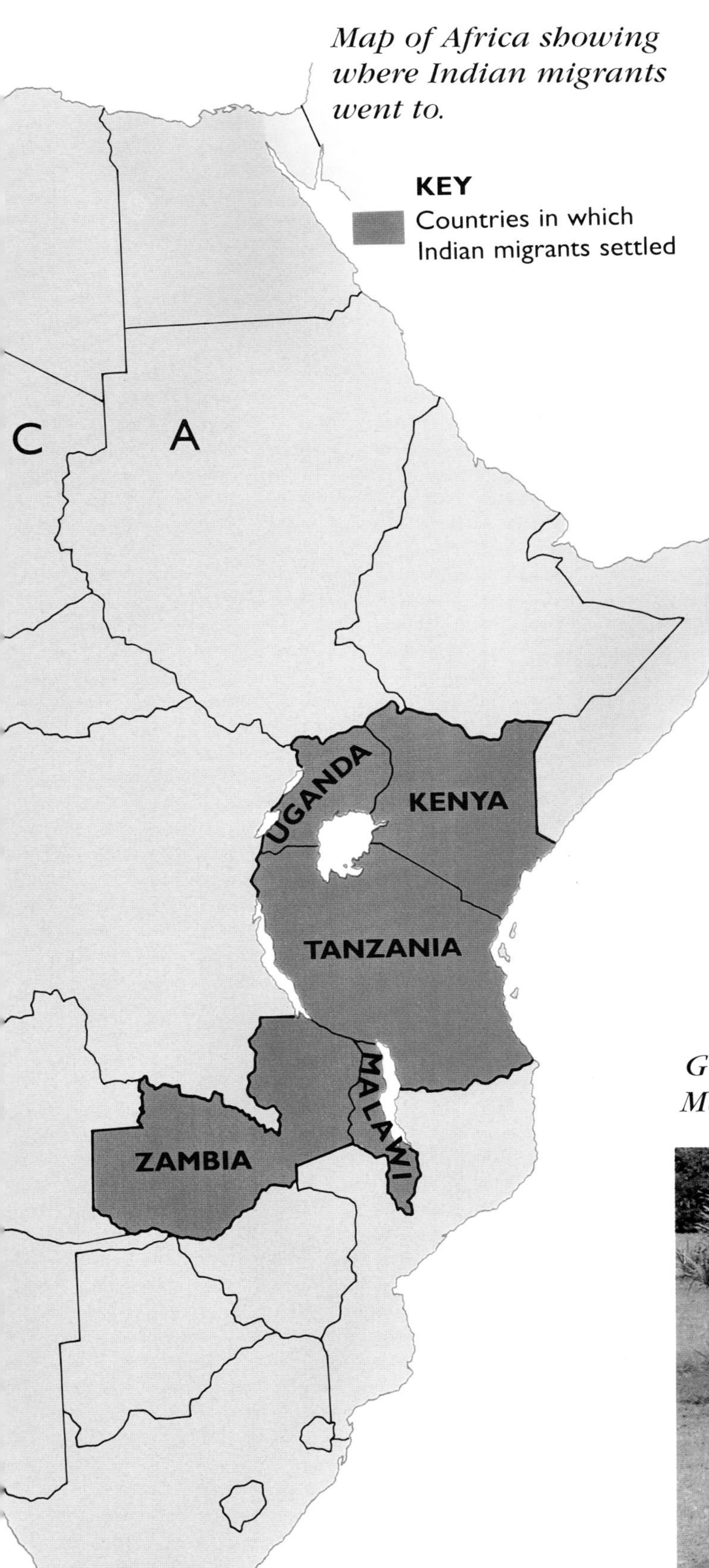

Map of Africa showing where Indian migrants went to.

'First, my uncle went to seek his fortune in Africa. He set up a shop in Uganda. He paid for the fare for his brother, my dad, to go out to join him. My father worked with my uncle all the time they were in Uganda, in a place called Mbale, near the border with Kenya.

'I was born in Mbale. I can remember the smell of my dad's shop so clearly – the spices, the bags of sugar and rice and chillies on the dusty floor, the big tins of oil. He also sold saris for Indian women so there were rolls of brightly-coloured cloth all over the place – pink and purple, jade green and vivid blue. The women would chat away in Gujarati and Kutchi as they chose their saris and the material for the tailor to make up into matching blouses.'

Gulshan and her family outside their home in Mbale. Gulshan is the woman in the front row.

When African countries became independent in the 1960s they wanted Africans to control more of the businesses and to have a greater role in running their countries. Africans resented the Indians' success.

Idi Amin, president of Uganda from 1971 to 1979.

The governments passed laws making it more difficult for Indians to run businesses. This was called 'Africanization'. Indians could become citizens of the new African countries, but many chose not to. They felt insecure and did not want to tie themselves to Africa. Africans resented this too.

Many Indians had British passports because India had been ruled by Britain until 1947 as a colony. Indians started to go to Britain, although after 1968 the British Government made it harder for Indians from East Africa to get into the country, even though they had British passports.

Gulshan continues her story:

'Idi Amin came to power in Uganda in 1971. In 1972 he said that all us Asians who weren't Ugandan citizens had to leave within ninety days. My husband and I only knew Uganda - can you imagine having to leave like that? We hoped we would be able to go to Britain because we had British passports.

'We went to Canada - Canada was more welcoming to some refugees than Britain. I think people in Britain were afraid too many Indians were going to come.

'In the end, Britain did take 29,000 Ugandan Asian refugees. Canada took about 6,000. It was terrible because we had to leave in a real hurry – Indians were being killed.

An Indian woman and her children being met by a friend at Heathrow airport, London, after fleeing from Uganda.

'We were only allowed to take £50 with us, and what we could carry in suitcases. I felt worse for my dad because he had spent all his life building up his business in Uganda, and all he ended up with was a suitcase of clothes and a few photos.

'We flew to London and then my husband and I went on to Canada. We've lived in Vancouver for over twenty years now. It has become home but I still think of Uganda a lot. I wouldn't feel happy going back though, after the way we were thrown out. That part of our life has finished for good.' [4]

Although Gulshan Parekh doesn't want to go back to Uganda, some Ugandan Asians decided in the early 1990s to go back. The government of Uganda under President Museveni encouraged Asians to go back and reclaim their property, and to put their money into the country.

Gulshan Parekh and her husband and niece in Vancouver, Canada today.

5 The lascars sail overseas

Many Indians left home in the eighteenth, nineteenth and twentieth centuries to earn a living as sailors on British ships. These sailors were called lascars. At first, the East India Company used Indian seamen to crew ships carrying goods from India back to Britain. From the middle of the nineteenth century onwards, different shipping companies used Indian seamen on their steamships.

An Indian lascar in a London dock, 1935.

These sailed between India and Britain from the 1850s until about 1950. The shipowners were keen to use Indian lascars as they could pay them much less than European sailors. They also thought that the lascars would find the heat in the engine rooms of steamships easier to cope with than white sailors. The lascars found the heat just as bad, of course.

Indian lascars hauling the anchor on board a British merchant ship, 1930.

INDIAN FOOD IN BRITAIN

English people also went, especially those who had been out to work in India for the Raj. They liked to eat curry and talk about their times in India.

A tandoori chicken dish.

The introduction of Indian restaurants to Britain has influenced the way British people eat. Many people now go out for an Indian meal, and buy curry powder or the individual spices (like cumin, coriander, turmeric, chilli and ginger) to cook Indian food at home. Most supermarkets sell an increasing range of Indian foods, such as chicken tikka, samosas, onion bhajis, popadoms, naan bread and prawn curry. In 1993 there were about 7,500 Indian restaurants all over Britain. Although they are called 'Indian' restaurants and serve typical north Indian food, like tandoori dishes, most of them are still owned and run by people from Sylhet in Bangladesh. Many have popular names like Taj Mahal, Kohinoor or Light of India, but a few have names that reveal their links with Bangladesh, such as Surma (a river in Sylhet), Rajshahi (a town in Bangladesh) and Sonargaon (an ancient city in Bangladesh).

6 Indians flee as refugees

India became independent from Britain on 15 August 1947 with Nehru's famous words: 'At the stroke of the midnight hour, when the world sleeps, India will awake to life and freedom'. India's independence was won after a long struggle by both ordinary Indians and famous Indians like Gandhi and Nehru. Indian people felt that they had the right to control their own country, and not be ruled by a faraway government in London. However, the success of achieving independence was spoiled by the outbreak of terrible violence in India.

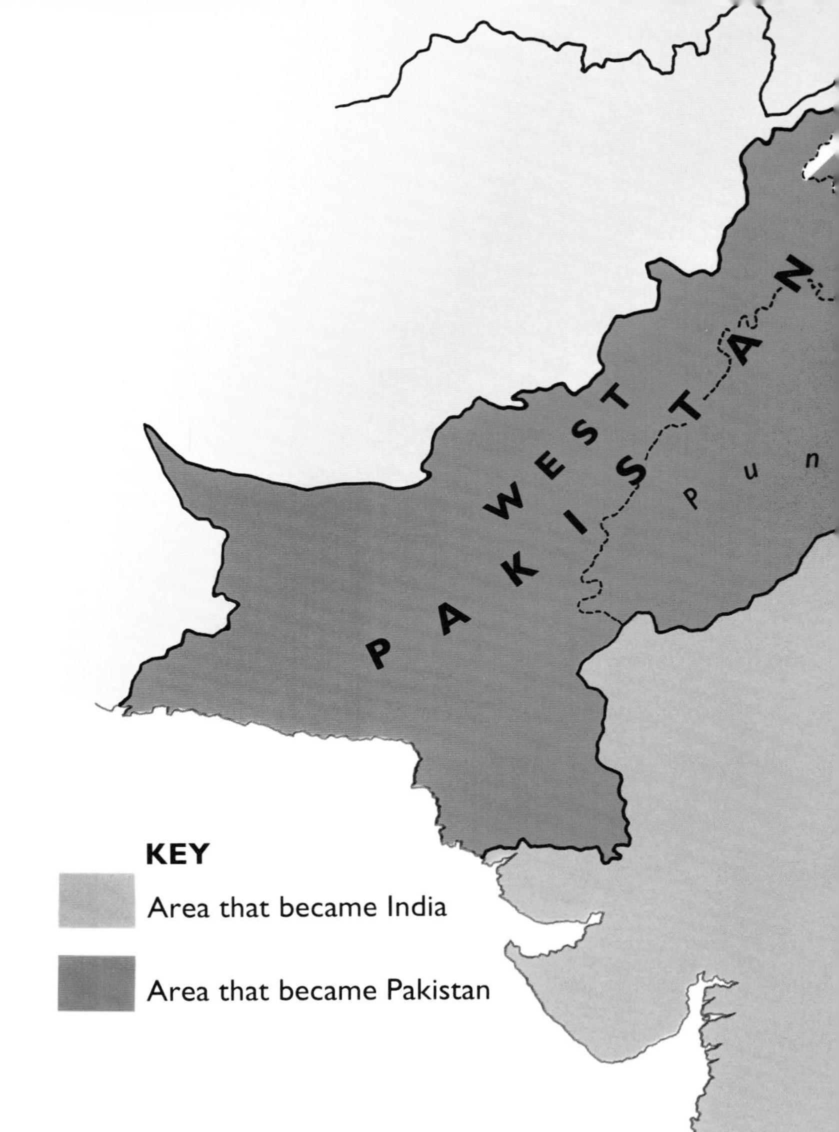

Most people in India were followers of the Hindu religion but a quarter of the population were Muslims. Muslims were involved in the struggle for independence from Britain alongside Hindus and Sikhs. But some Muslims were afraid that when India became free of Britain they would then be ruled by the Hindus instead of the British. One leader of the Muslims was Muhammad Ali Jinnah, and from 1940 onwards he demanded a separate country for Muslims, to be called Pakistan.

During the months before independence there were riots in India. Hindus killed Muslims and Muslims killed Hindus. Nehru and other leaders of the Congress Party (the main political party fighting for independence) reluctantly agreed to the partition (division) of India into two countries – India and Pakistan. They were afraid that if they didn't agree to it there would be a terrible civil war. The birth of independent India on 15 August was also the birth of the new Muslim country of Pakistan.

The partition of India, 1947

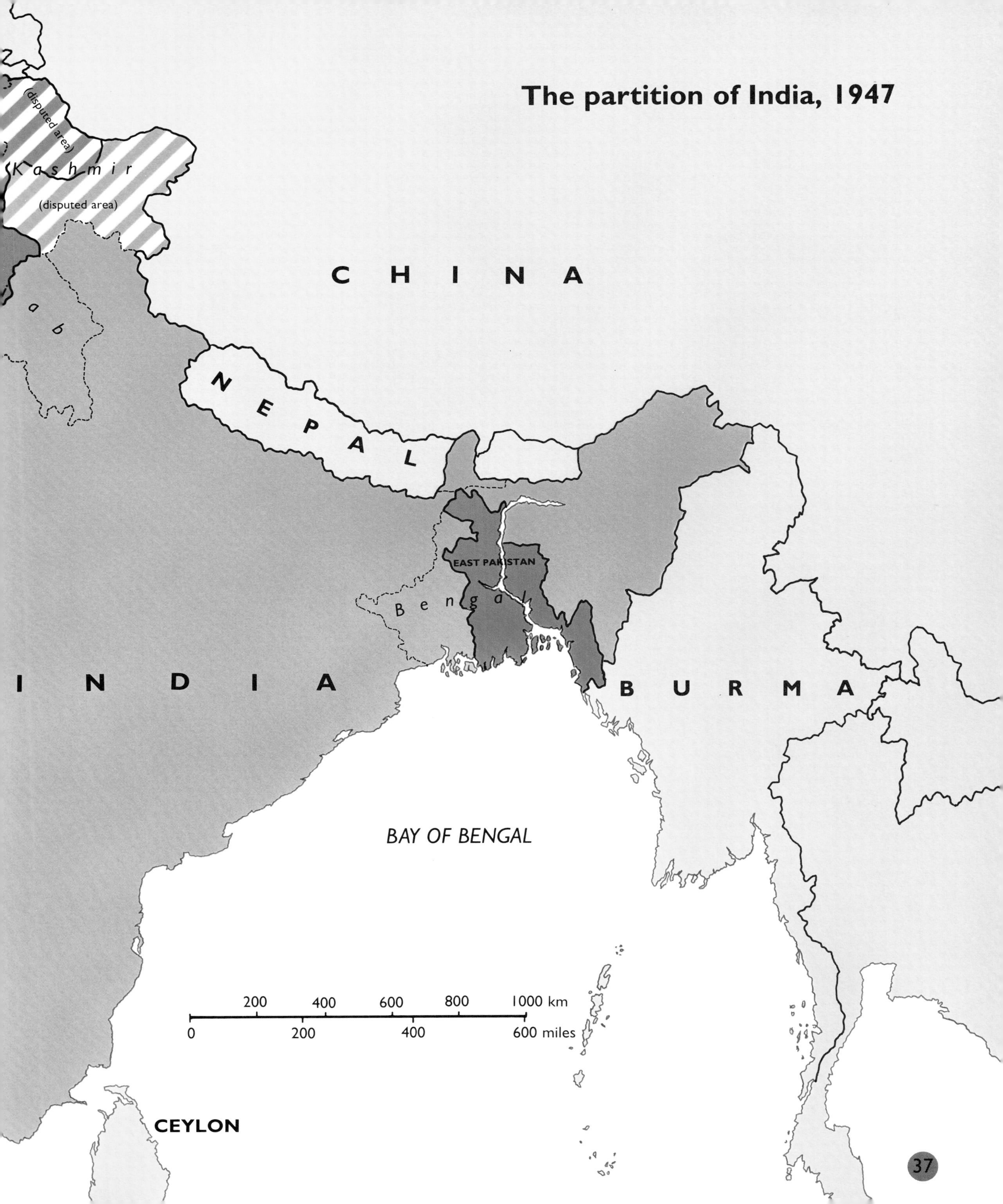

Pakistan was formed out of the two areas of India with a majority of Muslims – the north-west and east Bengal. These areas were about 1,500 km apart so Pakistan was made up of two separate parts – West and East Pakistan. (East Pakistan became the independent country of Bangladesh in 1971.)

When the new borders between India and Pakistan were drawn on the map, although Pakistan was mainly Muslim, there were still many Hindus and Sikhs left in West Pakistan and Hindus left in East Pakistan. There were also many Muslims left in India. As soon as the new countries were formed Hindus and Sikhs started killing Muslims in India, and Muslims started killing Hindus and Sikhs in Pakistan. Most killings took place in the Punjab, which had been divided between India and West Pakistan. The people there had lived side by side peacefully for years. But now, crowded trains carrying people to safety were attacked and the terrified passengers were hacked to death. Sometimes trains would roll into stations in an eerie silence because almost all of the passengers had been killed on the way. The final number of dead will never be known. One estimate is that about half a million people were killed.

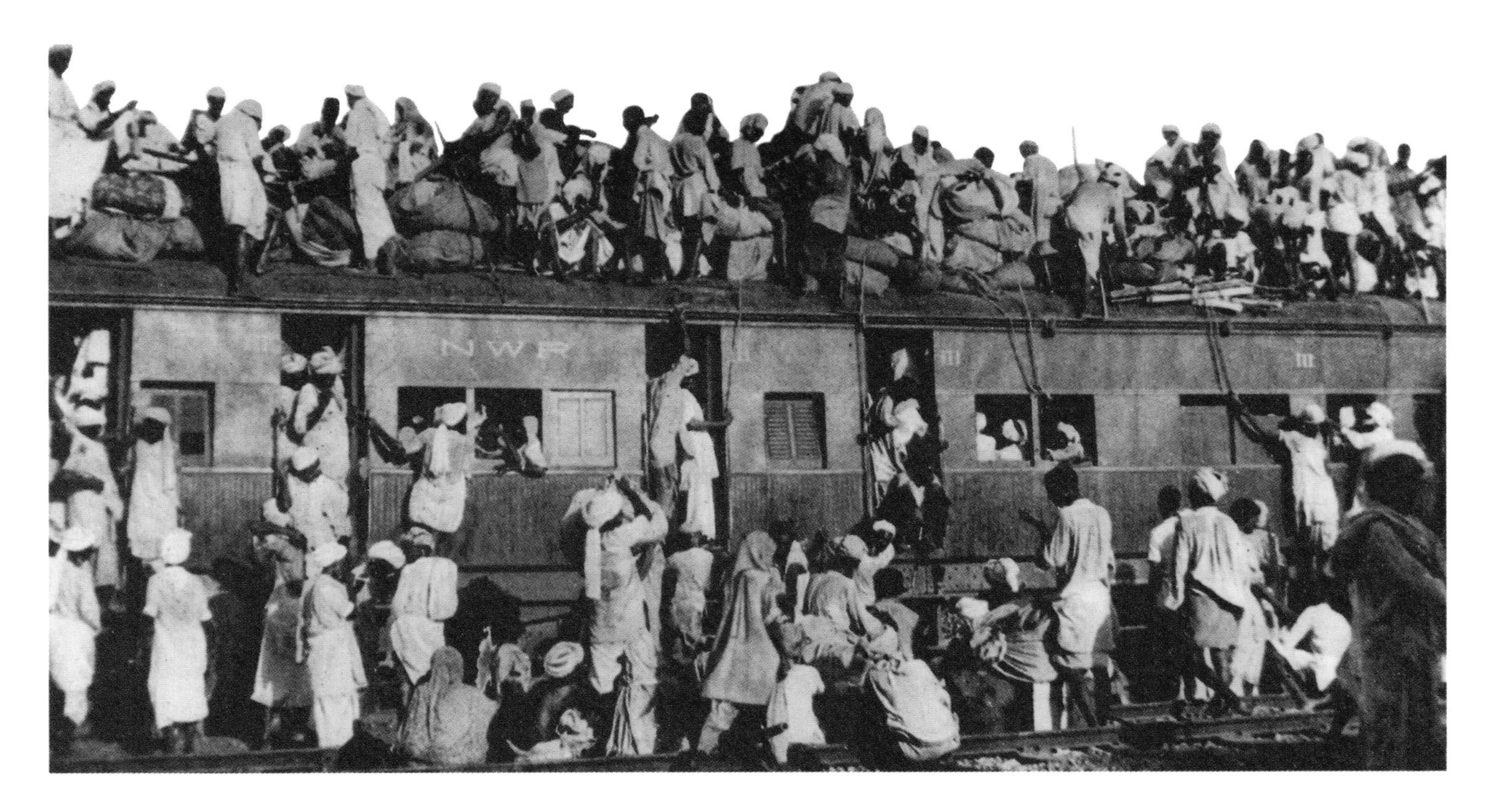

Muslim refugees, fleeing India on a packed train going to Pakistan.

The terrible violence in the Punjab meant that people decided that they had to flee as refugees to seek safety. Five and a half million Muslims in India moved across the border into West Pakistan and another five and a half million Hindus and Sikhs in West Pakistan moved the other way to try to find safety in India. They took whatever they could carry and went on foot, by bicycle, by train, by car, by bullock cart. Another million refugees moved from East Pakistan to India. This was the largest mass migration in history.

Destruction in Amritsar, Punjab, caused by riots just before the partition of India.

An Indian Muslim woman tells her story:
'We lived in a village in the Punjab. We had a small farm and grew rice and wheat. There were Sikhs and Hindus in our village and people got along fine. We knew about getting rid of the British but no one asked us about having a Muslim country. Why should we want a separate country when we'd always lived together? My husband told me that if Pakistan was formed the Muslims would believe that all the Hindus and Sikhs living there would leave for India. The Muslims would think it was their chance to get everything - all the Hindus' and Sikhs' houses and farms and everything. He was right - once Pakistan was formed, we heard that the Muslims there had started killing the Hindus and Sikhs. And then where we lived the Hindus and Sikhs didn't want us there, they wanted our land and houses for their relatives who had been driven out of Pakistan. So many people were killed, I can't bear to think about it too much. They killed my husband in front of me. My family had to leave, we had no choice.

'I took my cooking pot, some rice, two blankets and the family *Qur'an* and gathered up my three children and my elderly mother-in-law. We just walked. We were walking to Pakistan, a completely unknown place, leaving behind the village our family had lived in for centuries. There was a long line of refugees, stretching out as far as the eye could see. People were stumbling along, exhausted, with the sun beating down on them.

'People were carrying babies and those who were ill. Some people had carts with their possessions on. Sometimes the line of Muslims was attacked and yet more people were killed. Some died of cholera on the way. We often passed a line of Hindu and Sikh refugees going the opposite way. It was strange, some people yelled out horrible comments to them, but mostly I think we just felt sorry for each other and passed in silence. Finally, after waiting days, we crossed the bridge into Pakistan. We were safe, but all I could do was cry.' [6]

Hindu and Sikh refugees flock into Delhi from the Punjab, 1947.

7 Migrating to work abroad after 1947

Although India became independent from Britain in 1947, the link between India and Britain was not broken. After independence, people (mainly men) from India and Pakistan started migrating to Britain to work.

There were several reasons for this. Although people from Gujarat and Punjab in the west and north of India had always migrated, many more migrated after 1947 because these two states were on the new border between India and Pakistan. People were uprooted because of partition and lost their homes and land. This made some of them decide to go to Britain.

Another area which was affected by partition was Kashmir; the dividing line between India and Pakistan went through Kashmir. People have migrated particularly from the Mirpur area of the part of Kashmir which is controlled by Pakistan. When people migrate, there are 'push' factors, pushing them to migrate from their own country.

The partition of India was one of the 'push' factors. Another 'push' factor was that India and Pakistan were much poorer countries than Britain so people had the opportunity to earn far more money by working there. (The poorest people did not migrate, though, because they could not afford the fare.)

A Sikh man working in a rubber factory in Bradford, northern England.

When people migrate there are also 'pull' factors – things in the country they migrate to which 'pull' them there. In Britain the 'pull' after the Second World War was that Britain needed workers to go and work in its factories and industries to help rebuild the country. There were not enough British workers willing to work for low wages, so people from India and Pakistan were encouraged by the British Government to go and work in Britain.

Indians and Pakistanis worked particularly in textile factories and steel mills, and on the buses and railways. Although Britain needed them to do the jobs that British people weren't prepared to do, many British people were prejudiced towards the new arrivals.

In 1962 the British Government passed an Act of Parliament to limit the numbers of Indians and Pakistanis (and Afro-Caribbeans) going to Britain. From the mid-1960s it became harder for people without skills to get into Britain.

A number of other Immigration Acts have been passed since then to reduce the number of immigrants. Since 1971 the people arriving from India, Pakistan and Bangladesh have been the wives and children of men who had originally gone to Britain alone to work.

An elderly Sikh man tells his story: 'I came to Britain in 1952, with my brother. I was twenty-four. We had lived in the Punjab but it had been

Muslim children, whose families came from the Indian subcontinent, study the Qur'an *at this mosque in England.*

split in two, between India and Pakistan. We didn't really have enough land for everyone in our family. We Sikhs are great farming people – in fact later I bought some land in Punjab from my earnings in Britain – but when I was young I didn't mind doing something different.

Sikhs celebrating Baisakhi *– the first day of the Sikh New Year – at a Sikh* gurudwara. *The man is handing out sweets.*

'I heard they needed workers in Britain and we had British passports, so my brother and I came. We'd heard a lot about Britain because two of our older brothers had been soldiers in the British Army in India in the days of the Raj. Lots of Sikhs were in the army – we've always been a fighting people. My brother and I got jobs in a steel mill in the Midlands. It was very hard, dirty work and we worked long hours. We lived in a rented house with a group of Sikh men, all from our village in Punjab.

'In 1961 I went back to India and brought my wife and daughters to Britain. I'd managed to save enough money to buy a little terraced house for us to live in. My wife was very lonely at first and missed our village in Punjab. But some Sikhs started a gurudwara, a Sikh temple, in a disused chapel and we went there every Sunday, so my wife soon got to know other Sikh women. My wife and I are very religious and I still wear my turban even after all these years in Britain. It's not the same with the younger generation though – none of my grandsons wear turbans and they can't read or write Punjabi. They were born in Britain – I think they feel partly British and partly Indian.' [7]

The Indian, Pakistani and Bangladeshi people who have moved to Britain have taken their rich culture, traditions and languages with them. Many British towns and cities now have a Hindu temple, a Sikh gurudwara or a Muslim mosque. Different religious festivals are celebrated in Britain, like they are in India. For example, at the Hindu festival of *Divali* little clay lamps called *divas* are lit in Hindu homes.

The man in this picture is preparing for the Hindu festival of Divali.

Every year since 1987 there has been a big *mela* (outdoor festival) in South London, attended by thousands of people, both Indian and non-Indian. They watch classical Indian dancers and Indian magicians. People listen to Indian story-tellers, traditional Indian music and modern Indian music like rap and bhangra. They try Indian crafts like kite-making, hand-painting and embroidery, and eat Indian food – samosas, curries and tandoori chicken.

Many people from the Indian subcontinent who now live in other countries keep in close touch with their relatives who are still there. They phone and write to their relatives in India, Pakistan and Bangladesh, and many make regular trips to see them.

Migrant workers in the Gulf

An Indian waiter working in a hotel in Saudi Arabia.

In recent years people (again, mainly men) from India, Pakistan and Bangladesh have gone to work in the Gulf states (Kuwait, Bahrain, Qatar, the United Arab Emirates, Oman and Saudi Arabia). The Gulf states have needed extra workers since they raised the price of their oil dramatically in 1973–4 and have earned a lot of money so that they can pay for roads, airports, houses, schools and hospitals.

Most of the foreign workers have done building jobs. The small number of women who have gone have mostly worked as maids and cooks for Arab families. As with the earlier migration to Britain, people from India, Pakistan and Bangladesh have gone to the Gulf because they can earn far more money than they could at home. They then send this money home to support their families.

After the Gulf War of 1991 the rulers of the Gulf states no longer wanted large numbers of foreign workers. Many Indians, Pakistanis and Bangladeshis had to return home. Most are keen to migrate again.

As we have seen, throughout history Indians have migrated all over the world – sometimes happily, sometimes reluctantly – to try to improve their lives. Although there has often been conflict and suspicion, Indian migrants have greatly enriched the countries they have gone to with their cultural traditions, their languages and their skills and enterprises.

Glossary

Apartheid Means 'apartness'. It was the system imposed by the white government of South Africa in 1948 to keep white, black, coloured (mixed race) and Indian people separate, because of its belief that white people were superior.

Buddhist A follower of the religion of Buddhism, which was founded in India by Gautama Buddha and spread to other Asian countries.

Chain migration When people migrate by following earlier migrants from their area to the same place.

Citizen Member of a state. Citizenship involves rights, responsibilities and duties.

Civil war War between different groups of people within a country.

Colony A country which has been conquered by another state and is ruled by it.

Creoles Has different meanings in different Caribbean countries. It usually means those born in the Caribbean, but does not include Indians.

Descendants The relatives of people who lived many years ago.

Discrimination Treating a certain group of people badly because of negative feelings about their skin colour, language, religion or political beliefs.

Empire A group of countries that are governed by one ruling country.

Famine A severe shortage of food.

***Halal* meat** Meat from an animal killed according to Muslim religious customs and therefore pure for Muslims to eat.

Hinduism The most ancient of India's main religions. Hindus (followers of Hinduism) worship many gods. Vishnu and Shiva are the main ones.

Indentured labour A system whereby workers had to work for an employer for the period of the indenture (usually five years). It replaced slavery but was very similar to it.

Independent When a state is independent it can rule itself.

Jute Plant used for making sacks, mats and cord.

Kutchi An Indian language, similar to Gujarati, spoken by people from the area of Kutch between Gujarat in India and Sind in Pakistan.

Lascars Asian seamen.

Manual work Work done with the hands.

Mogul Empire The empire of the Muslim rulers who governed much of India for over three hundred years, from 1526 when Babur conquered Delhi and became the first Mogul Emperor.

Muslim A follower of the religion of Islam, founded by Muhammad, whom Muslims believe was a prophet.

Plantation Large farm, usually where one main crop is grown for sale abroad.

Prejudice Negative feelings about a group of people, not based on knowledge or facts.

Professionals People doing jobs which require a lot of studying beforehand, such as doctors, lawyers or teachers.

Qur'an The holy book of Muslims, which they believe was revealed by God to the prophet Muhammad.

Raj The period of British rule in India from 1858 to 1947.

Refugee Someone who has fled from his or her country and been accepted by the government of a new country because the person has a 'well-founded fear of being persecuted for reasons of race, religion, nationality etc'. (UN Convention on Refugees, 1951)

Sanskrit The ancient language of India, not spoken for many centuries but still used for some Hindu religious texts.

Sikh Follower of the Indian religion of Sikhism which was founded by Guru Nanak in the sixteenth century as an offshoot of Hinduism.

Sleepers Pieces of wood used to support railway tracks.

Subjects People who live under the rule of a government or monarch.

Find out more

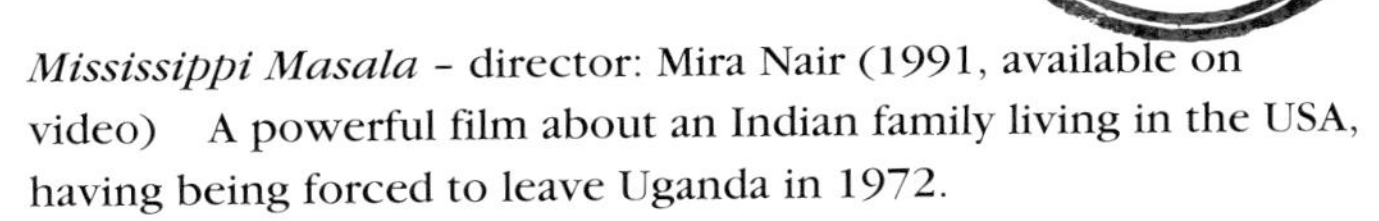

Books to read

Recommended reading age appears after each entry.

Chapter 1
Seasons of Splendour - Tales, Myths and Legends of India by Madhur Jaffrey, illustrated by Michael Foreman (Pavilion Books, 1985) Traditional Indian stories including an excellent re-telling of the Ramayana. 8–12

Chapter 2 (and Chapters 3 and 7)
How Racism Came to Britain (Institute of Race Relations, 1985) A cartoon book explaining slavery, colonialism, racism and the reasons why black and Asian people came to Britain. 11–16

Chapter 2 (and Chapter 5)
Indians in Britain by Rozina Visram (Batsford, 1987) Covers Indian migration to Britain from the eighteenth century to the present day, with many illustrations and extracts from documents. 12–16

Mahatma Gandhi by Michael Nicholson (Exley, 1987)

Chapter 4
Sumitra's Story by Rukshana Smith (Macmillan Education, 1985) A novel about Sumitra, a Ugandan-Asian girl forced to leave Uganda by Idi Amin, and her life as an immigrant in Britain. 10–14

Our Lives (English and Media Centre, 1979) Available from The National Association for the Teaching of English (NATE), 50 Broadfield Road, Broadfield Business Centre, Sheffield, S8 0XJ Autobiographical writing by young people including *Small Accidents* by a Ugandan Asian boy, telling the story of his life in Uganda and in Britain.

Chapter 5
A Taste of India by Roz Denny (Wayland, 1994) Indian food and recipes. 8–10

Chapter 7
Asian Voices - Life Stories from the Indian Subcontinent (Ethnic Communities Oral History Project, 1993, available from ECOHP, Shepherds Bush Library, 7 Uxbridge Road, London W12 8LJ) A collection of autobiographical writing by people from India, Pakistan, Bangladesh and East Africa who migrated to Britain. In Bengali and Urdu as well as in English. 12–16

Further information for teachers

Mississippi Masala - director: Mira Nair (1991, available on video) A powerful film about an Indian family living in the USA, having being forced to leave Uganda in 1972.

The following Minority Rights Group reports are available from the Minority Rights Group, 379 Brixton Rd, London SW9 7DE (071 978 9498):

East Africa's Asians: Problems of a Displaced Minority by Yash Tandon and Arnold Raphael (1984)

Indian South Africans by Frene Ginwala (1985)

East Indians of Guyana and Trinidad by Malcolm Cross (1980)

The Tamils of Sri Lanka by Walter Schwarz (1988)

Migrant Workers in the Gulf by Dr Roger Owen (1985, updated 1992)

Fiji by Hugh Tinker et al (1987)

Also from the Minority Rights Group: *Bangladesh is my Motherland by Rachel Warner* (1992) A case study of Bengali and English language development and use among a group of Bengali pupils in Britain.

A Place to Stay (Age Exchange, 1984) A collection of memories contributed by ethnic minority pensioners in Britain. It includes accounts by people from the Indian subcontinent and it is published in English as well as in minority languages. Available from Age Exchange, The Reminiscence Centre, 11 Blackheath Village, London, SE3 9LA (081 318 9105). Age Exchange also has reminiscence boxes (collections of objects) for hire, including one called *Born in the Indian Subcontinent*.

Ayahs, Lascars and Princes - The Story of Indians in Britain 1700-1947 by Rozina Visram (Pluto Press, 1986)

Across Seven Seas and Thirteen Rivers - Life Stories of Pioneer Sylhetti settlers in Britain compiled and edited by Caroline Adams (THAP Books, 1987)

Finding a Voice - Asian Women in Britain by Amrit Wilson (Virago, 1978) Now out of print, but still valuable, if it can be obtained.

A Language in Common by Marion Molteno (The Women's Press, 1987) A collection of stories based on the author's experience as an adult education worker, mainly among women from India and Pakistan.

V.S. Naipaul's novels set in the Caribbean, for example, *Miguel Street*, *A House for Mr Biswas*, and *An Area of Darkness*, a book about returning to India.